GETTING **Bullied**

SECRETS TO RESOLVING
CHILDHOOD INJUSTICES

Strategy Guide
by Katie Mann, LCSW

WE CAN DO IT TOGETHER

SHINING LION
CORPORATION

Address: GETTING BULLIED
             c/o SHINING LION PUBLICATIONS
             PO Box 74973
             San Clemente, CA 92673

Please refer to the website www.GettingBullied.com for additional information.

ISBN No. 9781439222058

Library of Congress Control Number: 2008943521

Check out the Shining Lion Website:

www.ShiningLion.com

TABLE OF CONTENTS

PART ONE: INTRODUCTION

PART TWO: BACKGROUND

PART THREE: TYPICAL BULLY

PART FOUR: GIRL BULLY

PART FIVE: CYBER BULLY

PART SIX: SIBLING BULLY

PART SEVEN: THE BULLIED

PART EIGHT: PARENTS

PART NINE: BYSTANDER

PART TEN: ALLIES

PART ELEVEN: EDUCATORS

GETTING BULLIED
Secrets to Resolving
Childhood Injustices

PART ONE:
INTRODUCTION

Beginnings

Handbook Structure

The Key Point

Book's Objectives

▷ BEGINNINGS

Bullying is a problem that spans all corners of our society.

GETTING BULLIED *Secrets to Resolving Childhood Injustices* strives to be the most accessible resource available today for anyone and everyone affected by this epidemic.

While there seems to be a tremendous amount of talk about this issue, we don't appear to have turned the corner on resolving the problem. There are still too many gray areas and uncoordinated efforts in addressing the issues, resulting in failing grades as a society.

What we must do at this critical point in time is to find new enlightenment regarding the problem along with new ways to finally win this battle, ultimately saving our kids and creating a better society.

▷ HANDBOOK STRUCTURE

"Getting Your PhD in Life"

This handbook is a key part of Shining Lion Publications' program that helps you achieve a PhD in life *(PhD = Personal Hands-On Development).*

GETTING BULLIED is written in a handbook format that makes information simpler to access and easier to understand. It is structured for action, with references to other respected sources.

This handbook is backed by the website www.GettingBullied.com. This additional resource will provide ongoing updates and access to other valuable assistance in this key area.

4

▷ THE KEY POINT

The bullying of our children is unacceptable.

Bullying has reached epidemic proportions in the last century. Almost 30% of the youth in the United States (or about 5.9 million) are involved in bullying others, being bullied or both.

Parents, teachers, administrators and children need to take a stand and stop this cruelty now!

▷ BOOK'S OBJECTIVES

GETTING BULLIED is the resource that will make a difference. It identifies the problems while offering constructive solutions to those problems.

This is straight talk that will make many feel uncomfortable while compelling others to take immediate, positive action.

GETTING BULLIED will do the following:

☑ Identify the obvious players in this drama

☑ Identify the not-so-obvious players and how they affect the drama

☑ Identify the playgrounds where these dramas take place

☑ Identify the problems and then present a do-it-now plan to help resolve those problems

In the end, the picture will be clear. GETTING BULLIED will offer tools to use and steps to take that will help change the way we handle this critical issue of bullying in our society.

6

Goals

- ☑ Bring new awareness to a critical topic
- ☑ Expose and stop the bad guys
- ☑ Create and recognize new heroes
- ☑ Offer comfort, protection, consequences and recommendations that will invoke the necessary changes
- ☑ Influence action: Individually, locally, regionally, nationally and beyond

The journey begins now...

PART TWO:
BACKGROUND

The Culture of Bullying in America

The Playgrounds

The Players

The Challenges

▷ THE CULTURE OF BULLYING IN AMERICA

Close your eyes. Picture yourself as an elementary school student playing on the blacktop. Suddenly, you see the meanest kid in school walking towards you. Your heart is pounding out of your chest because he is bigger and tougher than you will ever be and you know he doesn't like you. What will happen next?

Now, fast forward to high school. You are in a popular crowd and one of your friends decides she doesn't like you anymore. Rumors about you are flying around at school and the Internet. Soon, you find yourself eating alone and no one will come near you.

Bullying happens everyday all over the country, on playgrounds, on the Internet, even in the home.
Enough is enough.

We've all had at least one experience of being bullied and/or teased. While many of us were able to brush those incidents aside, surviving this childhood teasing and taunting, others have not.

Research concludes that prolonged bullying has serious long term effects on both the bully and the victim.

Bullying has historically continued to gain momentum to the point that it has now become an epidemic in our country.

According to a recent California survey (Knoll, 2001), a child is bullied every 7 minutes!

☑ 4% of adults intervened

☑ 11% of peers intervened

☑ 85% did nothing

What is happening to our children?

Why do the vast majority of our children who are being bullied end up being abandoned without support or help?

Many children are afraid to "tattle" to an adult for fear of repercussions by teachers, parents and especially their tormentor.

Several difficult questions must be asked AND answered if this problem is ever going to stop:

☑ Why is cruelty among children tolerated?

☑ Why are the numerous anti-bullying programs NOT working?

☑ Why are children not held accountable for their behavior?

☑ Why are so many of us standing around, allowing this to happen, lacking the right amount of empathy or knowledge on how to fix it?

> **We can no longer turn the other cheek and hope that our children will survive the mental and physical abuse at the hands of their peers.**

The Columbine tragedy, although obviously not justified, could be viewed as somewhat of a wake-up call. The young killers had been tormented by their peers for so long. They could not fight back with their bodies or minds, so they fought back with guns.

Unfortunately, there are other documented school shootings by students who were bullied over time with little intervention from schools, parents or peers.

The term "bullycide" has been used in relation to these stories. There's a good chance there will be more if our culture does not get bullying under control.

Paul Coughlin, the author of *No More Jellyfish, Chickens or Wimps (2007)* recently wrote about bullying:

"In order to help our children become confident, courageous and successful, we must confront this hideous form of treatment that if unleashed upon an adult would put the perpetrator behind bars. As it stands today, in part due to its prevalence, bullies, these purveyors of torment, are sometimes unlikely even to get detention!"

▷ THE PLAYGROUNDS

It's more than a push or a punch thrown on a playground.

We usually picture the interaction between the Bully and Bullied on the blacktop or a real playground.

Yes, this is a common battlefield, during recess or lunch, and just outside of the watchful eyes of a teacher.

That's only a part of the story. Some of these dynamics are actually happening in the classroom; peers making fun of a student's answer, passing notes, simply building a crescendo of subtle and not-so-subtle abuse.

There are now more sophisticated ways of putting bullying into motion, including cell phone texting, the Internet (email, Facebook, etc.). In fact, cyberbullying has become a major problem nationwide since the Bully can reach more people without ever having to face his victim.

There are other places where peers get together, including malls, dances, movies and sporting events.

Another recognized playground for this abuse is actually in the home between siblings. What should be the most comfortable place for a child, his home, can become an unsafe, even traumatic environment.

No matter where bullying takes place, either at school, on the Internet, at a ball game or at home, significant damage is done on all battlefields.

▷ THE PLAYERS

There are several different "players" in the drama of bullying. There are the Primary Players and the Secondary Players.

Primary Players

THE BULLY

This is the child that kids either fear or sometimes idolize. This child may be bigger, smarter or have a higher social status than his peers. Or simply, a disadvantaged child who chooses to bully in order to gain greater status amongst his peers.

The bully comes in different forms, including the Typical (most familiar one), the Girl (Mean Girl), the Cyber (online) and the Sibling (within your own home).

THE BULLIED

Also referred to as the "victim" or "target", this child bears the brunt of the assault. Some who are bullied handle this situation well, considering the circumstances, while many others who are bullied are left with long term scars.

The victim is often different in some way. He may be smaller, shy or have some other social limitations. His possible intellectual advantage lends itself to his social disadvantages.

Most of the time, he won't stand up for himself. There is "victim" or "easy prey" written all over his face. Studies show that there is a personality type for children who become victims of a Bully (Schwartz, 2000).

There are different personality types of victims, including Passive/Submissive (most common target) and Provocative (someone who brings attention to himself).

PARENTS

There are two primary types of parents, the PARENT OF THE BULLY and the PARENT OF THE BULLIED.

In many cases, the PARENT OF THE BULLY is a bully himself, lacking empathy, thus offering no help. Have you ever heard the phrase, "boys will be boys"? This is often a cover up that allows bullying to exist.

The parent of the bully is sometimes simply unaware, lacks knowledge on how to control his child, or underestimates the damage being inflicted by his son and chooses to do nothing.

On the other hand, the PARENT OF THE BULLIED may have a history of being bullied as a child. These parents tend to overprotect their child, often making matters worse. Other victims' parents either intentionally ignore the problem or don't know what to do about it, hoping the problem will go away.

BYSTANDER

The child who is bullied may not know how to ask for help, so it is the role of others to come to his or her aid. The victim's peers, parents and others such as school officials who ignore the obvious and less-than-obvious fit into this group.

To the bullied, this is a desperate battle. To those others who let it happen without helping for whatever reasons (i.e., fear, turning a blind eye, lack of empathy or knowledge on what to do), they are part of the problem.

ALLIES

This group can often and unfortunately be a part of the Bystander crowd, but most of the time they fit in this category as either a FRIEND or PEER.

They are either BULLY ALLIES or BULLIED ALLIES and play key roles for either side.

TEACHERS AND PRINCIPAL

They have a direct influence on the monitoring and management of bullying at school. Their roles in enforcing an anti-bullying program are usually significant.

Secondary Players
SCHOOL ADMINISTRATION

They run the school district and will oversee the implementation of a district-wide program.

SCHOOL WATCHERS

This group includes Parent Helpers, Playground/Lunch Monitors, Janitors and others).

Although not directly involved in the resolution of the problem, they have the opportunity to play important roles, depending on the situation. They are the eyes and ears for the other Educators as necessary.

AUTHORITIES

This includes PROFESSIONAL COUNSELORS and LAW ENFORCEMENT. These roles are utilized for the more serious problems, particularly law enforcement.

COMMUNITY

The INFLUENCERS encompass the rest of our society, those who are in the position to influence our children such as religious leaders, coaches and our friends' parents.

18

These ORGANIZATIONS include companies and other groups who can make an impact such as the PTA, Kiwanis, Rotary and Corporate America.

▷ THE CHALLENGES

Our goal as parents and educators is to provide a safe and fulfilling life and environment for our children.

However, there are a number of challenges facing us in this quest:

☑ Hold the perpetrators accountable for their actions while adjusting their future behavior to stop recurrences

☑ Turn all Players into <u>Backup</u>: these are the players who make a difference in supporting anyone and everyone who needs help

☑ Get all the Players to work together, creating a "synergy of effectiveness"

☑ Find a way to effectively and consistently empower those who can make a difference with powerful tools and a Plan

These are the challenges that must be met!

SUMMARY

Each player in the drama of bullying needs to be held accountable for his own behavior, actions or lack of action.

20

The drama will continue on our playgrounds, in our classrooms and other areas of our children's lives if something is not done to change the course of history of bullying.

We can work together to teach our children how to protect themselves with dignity and integrity. Our children look to us for guidance and protection. Let us take responsibility for our children's education as well as their future.

PART THREE: TYPICAL BULLY

Introduction

Common Traits and Behaviors

Why Do They Bully?

What is the Damage?

How Can Parents Help the Bully?

Sample Family Behavior Contract

▷ INTRODUCTION

MARK'S STORY

My name is Mark. It's not like I planned on becoming a bully. It started in the second grade when I was able to get lunches from friends just by scaring them. Now I can get almost anything I want just by threatening to hurt someone.

My home life is a nightmare. My mom drinks and my dad yells and throws things at her and at us. My brother and I used to hide but now I fight back or leave.

I know it sounds like an excuse but sometimes it feels good to be mean to other kids. I have a group of friends that hang with me but most of the kids at school are scared to death of me. I think it's kind of funny most of the time.

I have a lot of power at school. I eat other kids' lunches and they do my homework for me. It doesn't really matter. Nothing does.

If you or someone you love has ever been a victim of bullying, it is difficult to have much empathy for the bully. Studies show that a significant percentage of bullies are being bullied by either a parent or a sibling. (*Pacer Center, Inc., Marcia Kelly, 2005*)

Bullying is, in fact, a learned behavior. Many bullies seem self-assured and confident while others are tortured inside with no one to talk to. If our culture ever intends on controlling the issue, we must understand the bully.

DEFINITION

The description of a bully is not a complicated one. The dictionary explanation states: "a person who hurts or browbeats those who are weaker".

If you ask any child who has been bullied, his description of a bully might be the following:

"a kid who scares me and might hurt me"; "a mean kid"; "the boy who eats my lunch and takes my stuff"; "someone who says bad stuff about me to my friends".

Research varies on bullies. Some say that a bully is a kid with low self esteem while other research states that a bully is actually confident and believes that he is "cool and has friends". Either way, a bully is a child who physically, verbally and/or mentally takes advantage of other children that he or she perceives as weaker in any way. A bully attacks a weaker and often defenseless child. A bully enjoys the power he has over someone else. One thing is for sure: if you are being bullied, you'll know it!

▷ COMMON TRAITS AND BEHAVIORS

TRAITS

The following are some of the more common traits that a bully might possess:

☑ *The bully appears very confident and regularly brags about his conquests, about how mean he is to another child*

He continues to torment the child who won't fight back. Others won't go near the victim to help for fear of becoming the next target. This keeps other children from stepping in, thus creating the role of the "bystander".

☑ *The bully is often a "hothead", easily angered*

Everyone stays clear until they know what mood the bully is in. No one wants the verbal or physical wrath of this kid. Many times the bully comes from an alcoholic or abusive home where he has learned this behavior.

☑ *The bully often has little or no impulse control as well as low tolerance for frustration*

The bully may get in trouble at school for his impulsive decisions. This creates more frustration and he may take it out on others. If the bully feels "less than" in any area, he tends to act out against others in order to feel better about himself.

☑ *The bully will place the blame on other people rather than own his actions and behaviors*

It is easier for him to blame teachers, parents and peers for the poor choices he makes. You may often hear a bully irrationally and irresponsibly say that it was the victim's fault that he is being picked on, such as "he walked right in front of me so I had to give him what he deserved".

☑ *Bullies usually lack empathy for others*

The child that bullies usually cannot relate to what his victim is experiencing, lacking empathy and perspective.

☑ *Troubled home life*

Children and teens that come from homes with little or no emotional support are more likely to engage in bullying behavior (www.safeyouth.org). Children that come from homes where the parents are extremely permissive and lack involvement in their children's lives are at risk for aggressive behavior that leads to bullying. Extremely harsh parenting can lead to aggressive behavior in children as well. Bullying is a learned behavior.

☑ *The bully is often a coward*

One of the greatest problems with bullying is that it is not between two children of equal size and acumen. Bullying is almost always aggressive behavior from a more powerful child towards a child with lesser abilities to defend himself.

"This is why in many ways bullies are cowards: they launch their attacks of humiliation from a superior position with assurance of victory. The uneven playing field, tipped in their favor, emboldens them; bullies rarely go after someone of their own size in physical stature, verbal acumen, or social status. This is why adults must step in and level the playing field."

- Paul Coughlin, 2007

BEHAVIORS

The following are common behaviors/actions of a bully:

☑ *Teases and taunts his victim*

It empowers the bully to say mean things to another child; to feel better than and stronger than his target. The bully knows that at this moment, he is in control of someone else's life, and it feels good.

☑ *Uses physical force*

This includes kicking, shoving and punching to hurt his victim. Some bullies stop at taunting and name calling while others have been bullying longer or just have the need for the physical contact. At this point, the bully doesn't worry about the consequences of his behavior.

☑ *Damages or steals property*

This includes backpacks, lunches and homework, all part of a fun game for the bully. He watches the victim become frightened while obviously gaining something from this "transaction". He knows his victim won't tattle for fear that the bully will only make it worse.

☑ *Writes and distributes nasty notes about the victim*

Girls more commonly use these humiliating notes to start vicious rumors. Some bullies go to the length of pretending that the victim wrote the note about him/herself. In any case, it is meant to socially devastate the victim.

☑ *Makes the victim do things he doesn't want to do*

This can be viewed as a form of "hazing" similar to what takes place in college fraternities. The bully pretends that if the victim will perform certain acts, he will be allowed to hang out with the group, eventually being accepted. The activities can range from doing the bully's homework to something more dangerous that could cause physical harm. The bully will rarely, if ever, follow through with actually allowing the victim to hang out with the group. This leads to greater humiliation for the victim.

☑ *At higher levels of bullying, the bully will actually threaten to harm another family member or pet*

This can occur out of desperation if the victim does not obey the bully.

▷ WHY DO THEY BULLY?

Some of the reasons include the following:

☑ *Popularity*

The bully often feels his "power" gains him friends, the kids looking up to him. The truth is, many kids befriend the bully only to stay on his good side, avoiding being bullied themselves. Rarely does a bully have true, deep friendships since these relationships are actually based on fear.

☑ *Feeling of control*

The bully likes to be viewed as tough and in charge. This may be the only area of his life that he feels he can control. When the bully does not do well in school or other areas of his life, he feels that controlling others is a good thing. At least he is good at something.

☑ *Getting attention*

The bully may not get attention for anything other than his bullying. Being a bully makes others notice him and talk about him. He even believes that even bad attention is better than no attention.

☑ *Feeling of power*

Some bullies like to have others afraid of them. This makes them feel powerful and important. The look of fear on the victim's face actually makes the bully feel good, not remorseful.

☑ *Feeling of jealousy*

The bully might be jealous of his target because the other child is better than the bully at something (i.e. school, sports) or may have more friends. The victim may live in a better part of town or be more privileged. To bully is to be bigger and better than the victim.

▷ WHAT IS THE DAMAGE?

The damage created by the bully not only resonates at the school level but ripples throughout homes and the community at large. When children are afraid of each other and parents don't know what to do, we need to know who to turn to for support and guidance. That additional guidance must be available at a minimum through our schools.

Bullying has a direct impact beyond what we can see and feel. Bullying ultimately creates huge cracks in the foundation of our society.

Since the bully appears to be in control...we need a PLAN.

▷ HOW PARENTS CAN HELP THE BULLY

DISCIPLINE AND CARE

The only thing worse than a Bully is a Parent in denial that her child is a Bully. The Parent must admit the problem exists and address it effectively.

The Parent must teach that this behavior will not be tolerated in the family, in our schools or in our society, period.

TALK AND RELATING

Stay calm and listen carefully to the explanation. Do not come out of the gate angry and punitive or you will most likely not get the truth or the whole story. Do not immediately blame him/her for actions you do not know about.

If your child was bullied in younger years, he might be reacting by bullying others. Find your child's perspective, get to the root of your child's hurt, sadness and anger and ask the right questions:

☑ "How does it make you feel when you are mean to Johnny?"

☑ "Why do you feel the need to bully?"

☑ "Is there a reason you are picking on this one child?"

☑ "Do you have friends that join in with you?"

☑ "How would you feel if you were being bullied?"

☑ "How should you be treating other people?"

☑ "Are you willing to stop bullying and change your behavior?"

☑ "How can we help you stop bullying?"

If your child makes excuses, gets defensive, or even defends his bullying role, consider contacting School Officials or Professional Counselors for outside assistance.

If you were ever a Bully or Bullied as a child, describe your experiences. It's always helpful to share real world lessons as a mentor.

TEACH EMPATHY, RESPECT AND COMPASSION

Children who bully often lack the ability to understand how others might feel. Whether it's role playing or professional counseling, teaching this is critical for future behavioral change to take effect. You are likely your child's most important role model and she needs to see how you view this situation, how you treat others and what she can gain from this change in attitude towards others.

Children will gain more from inclusion versus exclusion.

Let your child know how important it is to respect boundaries, belongings and especially the feelings of others. Those who show respect get more respect.

Empathy and respect for others is imperative.

Praise your child when you see improvements.

KEEP VIOLENCE AWAY

Several studies have shown that allowing children to be exposed to violence does desensitize them to violence and makes violent behavior seem more acceptable. Most children can separate the make believe world from the real world, your child may not be one of them (www.SafeYouth.org, 2007).

SIGN A BEHAVIOR CONTRACT

This effective tool helps spell out expected behaviors and provides rewards and consequences for these behaviors. Ideally, sit down as a family and jointly devise a plan that can be immediately implemented. Another option is to utilize the services of a school counselor or professional counselor. Keep the contract simple, focusing on one or two behaviors at a time. Keep the rewards and consequences equivalent to the behavior, neither too elaborate or too strict, respectively.

▷ SAMPLE FAMILY BEHAVIOR CONTRACT

The following contract has been agreed upon by (family members names) on (date).

SCHOOL - Will maintain an overall B average in order to maintain his privileges; will turn in all of his homework; will work daily to obtain a C or better in Math.

HYGIENE - Will take a shower and wash his hair at least every other day (without complaining); will brush his teeth 2x per day.

BEDTIME - Will be in bed and ready to go to sleep by 10:00pm without arguing.

PHONE - May have 1 hour on the phone Friday, Saturday, and Sundays; may have 1 hour on school nights (Monday-Thursday).

DRUGS/ALCOHOL/TOBACCO – Absolutely no tolerance.

FRIENDS - May spend time with _____ for (length of time)_____ Attitude after each visit will determine if he can handle another visit.

RESPECT - Each member of the family will talk to each other with respect. There will be no name calling or threatening words from any family member. All family members need to use respectful language such as please, thank you, good morning, etc. when communicating with each other.

CHORES - Parents will not have to remind any child about his chores and each will complete his or her chores in a timely manner. (Clean room by 3pm Saturday, complete laundry by 3pm Sunday, trash cans brought in after school Monday). Consequences for not completing the chores include losing computer privileges and phone for one day. Rewards for completing the chores depends on each child, including extra hours out on weekend, dinner out, more game time....

MEALS - All meals will be eaten at the table with the entire family. Respectful language will be used and when anyone is ready to leave the table, this person will ask to do so politely.

This contract can be revisited at any time that all parties are willing.

Parent Signature_____

Parent Signature_____

Child Signature_____

NURTURE DREAMS AND TALENTS

A child Bully often has low self-esteem and lacks self-confidence. He feels the only way to have control in his life is to bully other children. Help your child develop healthy social skills by getting him involved in youth activities or other areas of interest. Self-esteem is developed when we feel that we are good at something and we can make a difference.

PART FOUR:
GIRL BULLY

Introduction

Different Types

How to Help the Girl Bully

▷ INTRODUCTION

*"What girls do to each other is beyond description. No
Chinese torture comes close."*   -Tori Amos

The competition between girls begins at a very young age.
Even in "mommy and me" classes, the competition starts
with who walks first, who talks first and basically how
perfect each and every little girl is. The moms that don't
buy into this and are there to enjoy their children are often
shunned or made to feel "less than" by the other moms.
Only the fittest survive. And so the game of "girl world"
begins. (Wiseman, 2002)

As little girls get older the game changes and as early as
first and second grade the girls that don't measure up are
excluded from the "cool" group.

These girls learn early about what it takes to belong. Some
girls with a strong sense of self can be excluded and go
off and find their own group, never to be bothered again.
However, many girls are destroyed by this exclusion and
learn that rejection hurts. The girls that have a hard time
moving on to other friends eventually find themselves
settling for whatever the cool group will throw their way.

These girls usually are the girls that are bullied and treated poorly by other girls. This group of girls, if not guided at an early age, can be set up for years of social isolation and bullying at the hands of other girls.

Most people picture the bully as the mean little boy that harasses other boys with verbal and physical threats. However, there is nothing worse than a mean, angry, spiteful little girl.

She can look you in the eye with a big smile while she is driving the knife into your back. The hardest part is that she rarely gets caught because she is so sly and manipulative and no one (especially her mother) will ever believe she could do anything mean...ever.

A NEW SURGE

She is usually smart, pretty and popular yet sweet. She flies under the radar with most parents and seems like she would never hurt a fly. But in the world of adolescent girls, the school bully wears designer jeans and expensive make-up. The girl bully is so powerful she can make other girls' lives so miserable that decades later they still have a hard time talking about it, if they can talk about it at all.

With the ground-breaking books *Odd Girl Out: The Culture of Hidden Aggression In Girls* by Rachel Simmons and *Queen Bees and Wannabees* by Rosalind Wiseman, there has been a surge of discussion and awareness about the bullying of girls by girls.

What was once a very hidden and not so believed phenomenon is now out in the open and girls are coming out in masses to talk about the abuse that they have tolerated at the hands of other girls.

For her book, Simmons interviewed hundreds of girls, some that described the bullying so bad that they developed eating disorders, transferred to other schools, used drugs and alcohol or became so depressed or suicidal that they had to undergo extensive counseling well into adulthood.

With boys, bullying incidents are intense and very painful but they are often more short lived and easily forgotten. "Not so for girls, who tend to use a kind of slow torture that is manipulative, calculating and sometimes even brilliant", states Simmons. Simmons labels this kind of bullying "relational aggression" or R.A.

This Bully uses the power of friendship and fear of losing one's social life as a weapon of destruction. This aggressive behavior includes starting rumors, giving the cold shoulder to punish another; breaking up friendships or threatening to stop being friends unless she gets what she wants. Many girls do whatever they can to avoid becoming be a victim of the Girl Bully.

The Ophelia Project "serves youth and adults who are affected by relational and other non-physical forms of aggression by providing them with a unique combination of tools, strategies and solutions". It has been in existence since 1997 and is one of the only "anti-bullying" programs specifically for girls in the country. Best selling author Simmons is part of the program and since her book was released in 2002 she has been inundated with calls and emails inquiring about the program and how to implement one in other schools and organizations. The project offers self esteem training and mentoring for girls. One of the most popular programs is called, *How Girls Hurt Each Other*. Older girls work with the younger girls and help teach and support them in their peer relationships. The program teaches the girls to set limits and boundaries in their relationships and helps them recognize when a relationship is not healthy.

▷ DIFFERENT TYPES

When working in schools, one of the first tasks of the Ophelia Project is to identify the dynamics in the room and put these girls into one of three groups: what they call the "aggressors", the "victims" and the "girls in the middle".

AGGRESSORS

The "aggressors" are more commonly known as the "mean girls", girl bullies or the queen bees of the crowd. From the beginning, these girls walk in like they own the place, have a crowd around them and usually tell everyone where to sit. Typically, they sit in the middle of their adoring entourage. These girls almost always are dressed to the "nines" and wear the latest designer labels, their hair and nails are done, presenting themselves as having the perfect life.

VICTIMS

The "victims", as stated by one of the project volunteers can also be identified immediately. "They look terrified, walk with their heads down, are very quiet and usually alone".

GIRLS IN THE MIDDLE

The "girls in the middle" are harder to identify but are the most powerful group of girls. These girls ride the fence and know in a moment's notice they could go from being "in" to becoming a victim themselves. These girls have a very low self esteem and often know what they are doing is wrong, they are just too afraid to stand up against the queen bee and become the next in line to be thrown out of the popular group.

For real change, these "girls in the middle" or "sidekicks", depending on the literature, are the group that is important to target. These girls usually have some knowledge of how wrong their behavior is and welcome the help to get out of the middle. Years later these girls may end up in therapy, trying to figure out how they were led into such destructive behaviors and how mean and hurtful they were to so many girls. The inability to take a stand against the bully for fear of becoming the "victim" makes them feel ashamed and many of the girls that were targeted by the Ophelia Project came back and volunteered as mentors.

▷ HOW TO HELP THE GIRL BULLY

Pay attention to this problem. Be aware of your daughter's mood and behaviors, and ask if something is going on. If you overhear something, gently raise your concern and let her know you are worried, that you are on her side, that you will not judge her friends or try to fix anything. Let her know that you are there for her.

Saying "I told you so" or refusing to let her hang out with certain friends will not work.

As a Parent, make sure your own past is not helping create a "Mean Girl" or enabling a Bullied victim. Teach your daughter how to fend for herself, how to navigate her more complex peer relationships with a supportive plan, even role play, if she is open to this help.

Do not go behind her back and contact other Parents or Teachers; do not overreact, even if she suggests to have the Mean Girl come over. Only when there is serious danger should you consider contacting Authorities.

Begin to understand Girl World (Wiseman, 2002):

☑ *Get involved in your daughter's life*

Learn more about her school, her friends and what she is doing with her time. Your daughter may not want you around but that should not be an option. When you know what your daughter is doing, and you know her friends and their parents, you have valuable information into how her relationships are going and who she is.

☑ *Set appropriate limits*

You are not her friend. Know where she is and who she is with at all times. Just because she is getting older and "all my friends are doing it" does not mean it is OK.

☑ *Promote honesty and integrity*

Listen and learn more about your daughter and her friendships. If you think your daughter may be a bully, ask. Listen to her feelings and gently advise her on how to handle the situation more appropriately. Encourage your daughter to apologize if necessary, an important skill to learn. Accepting responsibility and owning your behavior is the first step to not being the Mean Girl and bullying others.

**PART FIVE:
CYBER BULLY**

Introduction

Why Do They Cyber bully?

Different Attacks

How to Stop the Cyber bully

▷ INTRODUCTION

The Internet is not a safe place for our children. With technology becoming so advanced, what was once thought of as an advantage for our children has turned out to be a complete nightmare in many instances. The Internet can leave our children open and vulnerable, now one more playground where our children can be bullied.

Popular websites such as MySpace, Xanga and Facebook, to name a few, are the sites that our adolescents are gravitating towards. They want to be connected, to anonymously find out what is going on and even make new friends. At one point, predators were our big concern regarding these sites. Although this concern is still present, another growing concern is how our children are being treated by their peers on the Internet.

Cyber bullying and cyber harrassing are new terms and new issues on the upswing, causing psychological distress in our children and adolescents.

Most parents already feel overwhelmed with the job of parenting. Now, we must add to our job the monitoring of our children's access to the Internet. It is not acceptable that our children are navigating these dangerous "playgrounds" on their own. It is our responsibility as parents to protect them from physical and psychological harm, both potential dangers here.

Cyber bullying is described as, "willful and repeated harm inflicted through the medium of electronic text" (Patchin & Hinduja, 2006).

Cyber bullies are malicious aggressors who seek implicit or explicit pleasure or profit through the mistreatment of another individual. Violence is often associated with aggression, and corresponds to actions intended to inflict injury (of any type). One instance of mistreatment, while potentially destructive, cannot accurately be equated to bullying, and so cyber bullying must also involve harmful behavior of a repetitive nature.

Finally, due to the very nature of the behavior, cyber bullies have some perceived or actual power over their victims. While "power" in traditional bullying might be physical (stature) or social (competency or popularity), online power may simply stem from proficiency.

That is, youth who are able to navigate the electronic world and utilize technology in a way that allows them to harass others are in a position of power relative to a victim. There are two major electronic devices that young bullies can employ to harass their victims from afar. First, using a personal computer a bully can send harassing emails or instant messages, post obscene, insulting, and slanderous messages to online bulletin boards, or develop websites to promote and disseminate defamatory content. Second, harassing text messages can be sent to the victim via cellular phones.

CITATION: Patchin, J.W. & Hinduja, S. (2006). Bullies move beyond the schoolyard: A primary look at cyber bullying. Youth violence and juvenile justice, 4(2), 148-169.

SHARI'S STORY

It was just like any other day for Shari after school. She hurried through her homework so that she could get on the Internet and go to Myspace.com to talk to her boyfriend. Her parents knew nothing about this site and she told them she was doing research on the Internet. She talked for hours with "Tom" and shared her heart and soul with him. He told her he lived in Texas and was 16. Little did she know that "Tom" was really a 15-year-old girl named Tracy who went to her school. When Tracy had all the information she wanted, she posted it on every website she could think of and IM'd (instant messaged) it to all the kids at school. Shari was so humiliated by the incident, she refused to go to school and soon went to counseling for depression.

DEFINITION

Cyber bullying is when a child or adolescent is tormented, threatened, humiliated or otherwise targeted by another child or adolescent using the Internet or cell phone. It involves a minor on both sides, or at least have been instigated by minors. Once an adult is involved it is no longer considered cyber-bullying but is called cyber-stalking or cyber-harrassing.

This is not a one time incident but a repeated communication. Most teens are too afraid to get their parents involved and try to deal with it on their own. This usually doesn't work, often making matters worse. They know they should not have been spending so much time on these websites or IM'ing in the middle of the night. Therefore, teens are afraid of getting in trouble and rarely seek help before the situation has gotten out of hand.

SOCIAL CRUELTY

"Internet bullying has emerged as a new and growing form of social cruelty," Kirk Williams and Nancy Guerra of UC Riverside wrote in one of a series of reports published in the Journal of Adolescent Health. The reports, from researchers organized by the U.S. Centers for Disease Control and

Prevention, show a 50% increase, from 6% in 2000 to 9% in 2007, in the number of kids ages 10 to 17 who said they were online. *"Youth harassed online were significantly more likely to also report two or more detentions or suspensions, and skipping school in the previous year,"* Michelle Ybarra and colleagues at Johns Hopkins University in Baltimore reported in another study in the journal.

"Especially concerning, youth who reported being targeted by Internet harassment were 8 times more likely than all other youth to concurrently report carrying a weapon to school in the past 30 days," added Ybarra's team, who interviewed 1500 10-15 year olds. They found that 64 percent of those who reported having been bullied online were not victims of physical or verbal aggression in person. That makes for a whole new population of victims, the researchers agreed (Fox, M., 2007).

▷ WHY DO THEY CYBER BULLY?

Why do kids do anything? Because they can! As mentioned above, while the Internet provides many valuable things, kids can find a way to use something positive in a negative way. Adolescents cyber-bully for many of the same reasons they bully; power and low self-esteem.

☑ Motivated by anger, revenge or frustration.

☑ For entertainment or out of boredom.

☑ Many teens have too much time on their hands and too many toys to play with.

☑ No "guts" to do it in person; the computer gives someone the perfect way to deal with all of their feelings in the shelter of their own bedroom.

ANONYMITY OF THE INTERNET

"The anonymity provided by new technology limits a victim from responding in a way that may ordinarily stop a peer's aggressive behavior or influence the probability of future acts, which provides an advantage to the perpetrator." (Fox, M., 2007)

▷ DIFFERENT ATTACKS

There are two types of cyber-bullying; the direct attack and cyber bullying by proxy.

THE DIRECT ATTACK

Instant messaging/text messaging

Most teenagers have access to a computer or cell phone. Actually, most kids have their own. Kids send hateful or threatening messages to other kids without realizing the impact of these words on their peers. These messages can be very hurtful and because they are written and not spoken face to face, they can be taken the wrong way.

Creating similar screen names

A teen may create a screen name that is very similar to another teen's name by adding an extra letter somewhere in the name. He may use this name to say mean things about other kids while basically "posing" as someone else. This can definitely get the other kid in big trouble with peers.

Stealing passwords

A teen may steal another teen's password and post terrible

things on other websites. He can also lock the victim out of his own account.

Text wars

This happens when a group of kids gang up on someone and send hundreds of text-messages to the victim's cell phone. The victim is then faced with a huge phone bill and angry parents.

Sending pictures through email

There have been cases of teens sending mass emails including nude or degrading pictures of other teens. Once an email is sent, it can be passed along to hundreds of other people within hours and there is no way of controlling where it goes. This also happens with pictures taken on a cell phone in locker rooms or at a sleep over and then passed along for all to see.

Internet polling

Who's hot? Who's not...who is doing what with whom? These and many other questions are all over the Internet and are created by kids and teens. This is just another way to degrade, embarrass and bully other kids online.

Websites

Children used to only tease each other on the playground. Now, kids can create a website that may insult or endanger another child. They can create pages to insult another kid or group of people. They can also include identifying information that can put a teen at risk of being found or contacted.

Hacking

There are many teens that are so good at technology they can hack into another teen's computer. They can send viruses or spy on their victim. Trojan Horse programs allow the cyber bully to remotely control his victim's computer or potentially erase the hard drive of the victim.

Impersonation

There is software available that allows someone to impersonate another person. Posing as the victim, the cyber bully can do major damage. They may post a provocative message in a hate group's chat room posing as the victim. They may provide the name and address of the victim to make the hate group's job easier. They have no idea how much actual danger they are putting their victim in, nor do they usually care.

ATTACK BY PROXY

Jennifer was desperately jealous of Vicky. Vicky had it all; the looks, grades and the boyfriend. After Vicky didn't invite her to a party, Jennifer planned a vicious cyber attack. She went online posing as Vicky and posted, "I hate Meagan. She is stupid, fat and ugly and she is trying to steal my boyfriend. I want everyone to ignore her". Jennifer then called Meagan and told her that she had read these insults on MySpace and she had better hurry to see it for herself. As a result of what Jennifer created, Meagan and her friends started attacking Vicky and got the whole school involved. Everyone else was doing Jennifer's dirty work for her while Jennifer sat back and watched Vicky's life unravel. Vicky became the victim of cyber bullying while her peers harassed her for "mean behavior" that never even existed.

The above scenario is very typical and is called "cyber bullying by proxy". This is when a cyber bully gets someone else to do the dirty work for them. This type of cyber bullying can be very serious and there have been cases of suicide and homicide connected with this kind of Internet misuse. (www.stopcyberbullying.org, 2007)

Teenagers are unaware of the risks they take when they use a computer, especially in the many chat rooms and websites that interact with other peers. It is not that difficult for someone to get access to a password or gain control of someone's account information. The cyber bully can also change the password so that the owner of the account can no longer access his own account. Many people have been kicked off these sites for unacceptable behavior when they were not the ones doing the postings.

To take it even further, some cyber bullies post information about their victim in a hate group chat room or discussion board. They will pose as the victim and say terrible things about that particular group. The bully can leave personal information about the victim so that the hate group can find him.

The bully has no idea (or maybe he does) the danger that he is putting the victim in. There have clearly been homicides as a result of this type of Internet abuse.

If your child ever feels that he has been a victim of this type of attack, you must call the law enforcement agency immediately and take the threat seriously.

COMPUTER OVERUSE

One primary concern about the computer and Internet is that it may be keeping your child away from the real world.

"My life became completely unmanageable my junior year of high school. I had a MySpace site and was on the computer for hours after school every day. It was so much fun to talk to my friends and meet new people. After awhile I was so involved that I ended up having only an online social life. My friends and I would fight and make up and my life was miserable.

"Then the bullying started. I liked a boy that someone else liked and the other girl would post nasty, threatening things about me every day. People at school would read them and believe her and I became known as the "slut" at school. I couldn't tear myself off of the computer and my grades slipped down to Ds and Fs.

"My parents had no idea what was going on and by the beginning of my senior year, I had no hope of getting into a good college. I had very few "real" friends and was lonely and depressed. I started going to counseling and it helped me discover I was actually addicted to the computer. It took awhile and a lot of support from my parents, but I finally deleted my MySpace site and began to get my life back.

"I have such regret that I wasted most of high school years by spending countless hours online. I now go to high schools *and talk to other kids about computer addiction and being bullied online. It is amazing how many kids are in the same situation."*

Teenager (Kelly, 18)

▷ HOW TO STOP THE CYBER BULLY

The first step in eliminating cyber-bullying is to acknowledge that there is a problem. As mentioned earlier in the chapter, kids don't want to tell parents about problems on the computer, fearing their computer time might become limited or taken away altogether. Explain to your child that you will work with them but also need to know what is going on so that you can keep them safe.

Most of "what to do" depends on the situation. Have your child ask themselves the following questions:

☑ Am I in danger?

☑ Are these issues adding stress to my life?

☑ Is the computer taking away from other areas of my life?

If there is any danger it is important to act immediately. Again, depending on the situation, you may have to get authorities involved. This most likely will occur if there are any threats involved and how serious they are. Another reason to get the authorities involved would be if any credit card, social security number, etc. have been obtained and could be used by other people.

If your child is being bullied or harassed through her email, it will be time to delete this email address and get another one. Have your child give this address out *only* to her close friends and others she can trust. If the cyber bully obtains this address, it will be mandatory that your child take a break from the computer for awhile until the cyber bully moves on, unfortunately, to another victim.

Before you delete anything, print any evidence for proof if needed, at a later time. At some point the authorities, a teacher or principal, or the other child's parents may need to see proof of the harassment.

If there is any bullying through a website such as Facebook or Myspace, alert the website and have your child delete her page immediately. At a later date, when the dust settles, your child can recreate her page if she so chooses. Usually after a break from the drama, many teens decide to stay off of those sites and avoid the problems altogether.

If your child gets off of the computer and the cyber-bullying continues through another friend's site, particularly if it is a peer, it must be reported to the principal at his school and documented. In most of the cases, when the teen gets off of the computer and takes a break, the cyber-bullying will stop.

64

The most important thing is communication with your teens about this issue. You want to have open dialog about your concerns as well as their concerns when it comes to the computer.

If your child refuses to get off of the computer and the bullying or harassing continues, you may have no choice but to take the computer away and force a break. Your child can use the computers at school or the library for homework. All children need to learn their limits and be able to create balance in the different areas in their lives. At some point, parents need to take a stand and make sure their children learn this valuable lesson.

PART SIX:
SIBLING BULLY

Introduction

Why Do Siblings Bully?

The Dangers

How to Help the Sibling Bully

▷ INTRODUCTION

SAM'S STORY

I have feared my brother for as long as I can remember. I spent most of my childhood years hiding from him and trying to stay out of his way. For no reason at all, he would threaten me. He once punched me so hard he knocked the wind out of me. He would also leave bruises on my arms in just the right place where no one would see them. Besides constantly being mean to my dog, one day my brother killed both of my goldfish when I didn't do what he wanted me to do. I would give him my food and he would steal things from my room. It was never enough. I didn't tell my parents because he would have gotten in trouble and that would have been the end of me. To this day, I truly believe he hated me and would have hurt me. As an adult, I have no relationship with my brother and feel so much anger towards my parents for not being more aware of his bullying. Needless to say, it has taken years of counseling to unravel the issues of low self esteem and anger that I have held inside since my childhood. Home should be a safe place and no one should have to live in fear of his brother.

THE BULLY IN YOUR HOME

The sibling relationship is a powerful one. Much of our self-worth and self-esteem comes from our relationships with our brothers and sisters. When sibling rivalry turns into bullying, there can be life long relationship and self esteem issues. When parents turn the other cheek and let one sibling bully another, they are setting themselves up for years of problems within their family.

It is the parent's responsibility to make sure that siblings are kind to each other and treat each other with dignity and respect. This is not to say that siblings will not argue and fight with each other. This type of relationship when handled correctly can teach children how to address conflict and compromise in relationships.

However, when sibling rivalry crosses the line and becomes bullying, as it does for 30% of children, parents need to step in and intervene (*Schifferdecker, 2007).*

Each child reacts differently to teasing. What one child finds funny, another may find mean. If one of your children is constantly upset or feeling bullied by the other child it is time to step in. If your child that is bullying states that he is "just teasing", you must explain that not all teasing is fun or funny and teasing can hurt people.

▷ WHY DO SIBLINGS BULLY?

The following are some questions that you may want to ask yourself as you are trying to figure out where the sibling bullying is coming from:

☑ *Does the bullying child have issues with self esteem? Is he jealous of the sibling he is bullying?*

Many times sibling bullying begins as sibling rivalry and will get out of control over time. If the child that is being bullied is smaller, weaker, or looks up to the older sibling, they may be tolerating more than they should.

☑ *Has your child had any major changes in his/her life over the past few months (death, divorce, move)?*

Your child may be acting out his feelings and frustrations on anyone that will take the abuse.

☑ *Has your child's social life changed at school or in the neighborhood?*

The power of friendships during these years is huge. If someone is being mean to your child or is leaving them out of a circle of friends they may not know how to deal with these feelings and may be taking their feelings out on someone younger or weaker.

☑ *How is your child's home life?*

Your children may be crying out for some structure and attention. If sibling bullying persists, there will be long term detrimental effects on both the bully and the victim.

A HEALTHY FAMILY LIFE

Ideally, your home and family should be a safe haven. Home is the place where after a long day you can walk through the door and immediately feel loved and safe. You should be able to look forward to coming home at the end of the day and feel happy to be with your family. Unfortunately, some children dread coming home and would rather be anywhere else. Sometimes it is the parents that argue and bully each other, or a parent will bully a child, or a sibling will bully another sibling. Any of these scenarios is not what we would refer to as a healthy family.

Even in a family situation that is not so extreme there could be problems of bullying. A more permissive parent may allow bullying to occur without realizing it. Many adults were bullied by their siblings and feel that it is a normal "rite of passage" of childhood. The parent that feels this way may actually encourage bullying between siblings and may unknowingly reward the bully for being tough and strong with positive attention. Meanwhile, the child who is targeted will withdraw and feel that he is "bad" for being "weak". Rather than being taught how to respect each other and work as a team, siblings are set against each other.

Children in general are rather selfish. When left to deal with situations on their own, usually they won't think of how the other child may feel. They are out for themselves.

As children get older, the sibling relationship is much harder to control.

▷ THE DANGERS

The clearest long term effect of sibling bullying is the breakdown of the family unit and the irreparable damage that is done within a family. Bonds are either never formed between siblings or end up broken after years of torment at the hands of someone that is supposed to be trusted.

Self esteem for the victim is obviously an issue but that is true for the bully as well. Often times, after years of bullying and family discord, the bully is able to see the damage that has been done and has remorse for the destruction that he has caused his family.

We may blame society, the schools or other children for bullying, but we must first look much closer and examine our own homes. Parents must take responsibility for the relationships between themselves and their children. If we are ever going to get a handle on the devastating effects that sibling bullying has, not only on our own children, but on the very foundation of our family, we must first look in the mirror and do the work it takes to create a loving, gentle family home life for our children to thrive in.

Protect the home first.

▷ HOW TO HELP THE SIBLING BULLY

Make sure each child knows the household rules. Name calling, threatening or hitting should never be tolerated.

Appropriate consequences should be adhered to and consistently enforced.

Assist each child with the ability to understand and handle his feelings. Teach him how to better express his frustration, disappointment and anger.

Make sure that all members of the family treat each other with kindness and respect. If parents bully each other or bully the children, it is more likely that their kids will bully each other as well.

Each child must accept responsibility for his own behavior. Hitting, punching or kicking should never be tolerated in your home and a firm consequence should be given every time a child touches another child in anger.

Instill and enforce fair play, empathy for others and mutual respect among siblings.

**PART SEVEN:
THE BULLIED**

Introduction

Understanding the Victim

Common Traits

How to Help the Bullied

▷ INTRODUCTION

CODY'S STORY

It was like any other day for Cody Smith, age 12. He woke up and told his mom that he felt terrible, trying one more time to stay home from school. He couldn't tell her why he hated school, she would go talk to the teacher and that would make it worse. After begging her to let him stay home, she made him go to school. He dreaded getting out of the car.

The three boys always knew where Cody's mom would drop him off and they would be waiting for him. The harassment would begin immediately, eventually throwing his books in the bushes and taking his lunch.

Cody hoped the teacher would let him eat lunch in the classroom, but he usually had to go to the lunch tables. He often starved since he didn't have any friends that would share their lunch with him.

Some days, the boys would leave him alone and other days they would tease, kick and sometimes push him down. There were no other kids brave enough to help and he knew that the teachers would just look the other way rather than deal with the boys and their parents. Cody's life felt hopeless. He thought about ending it all rather than have to go to school even one more day...

▷ UNDERSTANDING THE VICTIM

Cody's story is one of thousands of stories told by children dealing with bullying. It is absolutely no wonder why after years of being tormented by their peers, many victims become anxious and depressed. Several documented cases have proven that teen homicide and suicide have come from this prolonged anguish and maltreatment.

"Nearly 90 percent of third through sixth graders experience some degree of victimization by bullies and 59 percent admit to bullying others" a new study by California research shows. *"This doesn't necessarily mean that 90 percent of kids are victimized to the extent that they are going to have serious consequences. The results do underscore the importance of finding effective ways to prevent bullying and victimization among children, which can indeed have serious mental health consequences for some kids."*

- Dr. Thomas P. Tarshis, Bay Area
Children's Association (May 2007)

DEFINITION

The definition of "victim" in the Webster's dictionary is:

*"someone or something killed, destroyed, sacrificed, etc.; one
who suffers some loss, especially by being swindled"*

The words "destroyed" and "sacrificed" fit perfectly. Bullying
slowly erodes the soul of the victims and does destroy their
sense of self-worth and self-esteem.

For many victims, lack of peer relationships, declining school
success, and overall hope for the future is so destroyed that
life seems empty and hopeless. This is the description of
"victim". Any parent who has had to watch his child deal
with being bullied knows this is true:

*"Joel was a happy, healthy young child. He often played
alone and didn't have many friends, even as a toddler. When
he started school, he was clearly different from the other
children. He played alone and did not interact with others.
The bullying began almost immediately. The boys would tease
and taunt him. After they realized that he was afraid, they
would actually push him and throw things at him. As early
as first grade, he began refusing to go to school. I watched my
beautiful, smart child slowly deteriorate in every area of his
life. How is it possible that a 6-year-old can be depressed?
My heart was broken and I felt like I had nowhere to turn."*

- Parent of a first grade victim
of bullying

▷ COMMON TRAITS

No one wants to be a "victim" of anything. The word "victim" itself connotes weakness and passivity. As parents, we hope and pray that our children will be strong enough to withstand any bullying that they may have to endure throughout their childhood. We want our children to be confident and make friends easily. The first time our child comes home crying and telling us that they were pushed down and had their lunch stolen, our blood boils.

We immediately want to come to the rescue of our children and confront the Bully. As difficult as it may be, we need to look at our children objectively and make sure that we are not setting them up to be bullied. As much as there is a "profile" of a child that bullies, there is a "profile" of a child that is bullied as well. (Schwartz, 2007)

As a culture, we think we know and understand the typical victim of bullying. Some of the characteristics of the "classic" victim are the following:

☑ Timid and shy/socially awkward

☑ Anxious/insecure

☑ Physically different than their peers

☑ Cautious

☑ Low self-esteem

☑ Socially isolated/lacks social skills

Typically, victims are usually children who can be overpowered either physically, socially, or emotionally by the bully. As mentioned above, these children often have low self-esteem and have trouble making friends. They do not feel confident in themselves and sometimes feel stupid and worthless. They are often lonely, friendless and alone at school, even reporting dislike of school, especially during recess or gym time.

In his pioneering research on bullying behaviors, Dr. Dan Olweus has described two types of victims:

THE PASSIVE (OR SUBMISSIVE) VICTIM

☑ Is non-assertive and through his actions may signal to others that he is insecure and won't retaliate if attacked or insulted

☑ Is cautious, quiet or anxious

☑ Cries easily and collapses quickly when bullied

☑ Has few friends and isn't connected to a social network

☑ Lacks humor and pro social skills

☑ May be physically weak

THE PROVOCATIVE VICTIM

☑ Is both anxious and aggressive

☑ May cause irritation and disruption around him

☑ Is easily emotionally aroused

☑ Prolongs the conflict even when losing

The above profiles have been adapted from *Bullying at School.* Many kids with Hyperactive/Impulsive AD/HD are provocative victims because they say impulsive things, tend to annoy their peers and over-react to bullies. Some children are bullied for no reason, while others are bullied because they are different in some way, either the way they look or the way they behave:

☑ The way someone talks or walks

☑ The color of someone's skin

☑ Physical appearance (fat or skinny)

☑ Their name (for example, a name that rhymes with a bad word)

☑ They have a learning disability or are different academically

☑ They act weak or scared or cry often

☑ They seem anxious and unsure of themselves

☑ Usually view themselves negatively

They feel lonely and friendless and usually are alone at school.

The bully can almost smell weakness in another child. These behaviors and traits are usually apparent at a very young age. It is important as parents and educators that we are able to detect and correct these behaviors as early as possible so these children have a fighting chance at a normal and violent free childhood.

▷ HOW TO HELP THE BULLIED

If you have read the warning signs and have concerns that your child is being bullied, take immediate action. The first step will be to talk to your child and obtain as much information as possible. Let him know that he is not in trouble and that you will not over react but will take immediate steps to remedy the problem.

After you have found out what is happening and who is involved, it will be important to talk with your child's teacher or school counselor, depending on your child's grade level. Inform them of what is going on and ask for immediate intervention. Ask the teacher to take a stand and set firm limits with the child that is bullying your child. Consequences of continued bullying should be made clear and the incident and discussion should be documented with a copy given to the principal.

Discuss an appropriate plan with your child and the teacher detailing what your child should do if the bullying does not stop. Make sure there are safe places and other adults that your child can turn to if he needs support. Ask if he can come back to the classroom at recess or lunch if at any time he does not feel safe. If this is not an option, insist that he have a safe place to go at all times if needed. If your child sits by the bully and would feel better if his seat was changed, request this. If the bullying does not *immediately* stop, you must take the issue to the principal and ask for intervention at this level. Request a meeting with the other parents and inform them of what has transpired between the children. Once again, ask that the principal firmly take a stand and delineate consequences and follow through with them.

Monitor the progress daily and make sure your child begins to feel safe again. An important issue that cannot be overlooked has to be discussed. Is your child constantly being bullied by other children? Is he easy prey for the mean kids to pick on him? If so, individual and family counseling is warranted and can help teach your child how NOT to be a victim of bullying.

Other options include:

☑ Social skills classes

☑ Assertiveness training

☑ Martial arts/sports to develop strength and confidence

☑ Find an older child to mentor your child (*see BULLEAVE*)

Do NOT ignore the warning signs. If done correctly, you can protect your child and at the same time teach him how to protect himself. This skill is essential for the development of a healthy self-esteem and will not only serve your child now but throughout his entire life.

**PART EIGHT:
PARENTS**

▷ INTRODUCTION

WHAT'S GOING ON WITH YOUR KID?

A parent's role is critical in keeping a child's life on track, stress-free at school and elsewhere. There are many things a parent must look out for, understand what the problems are if any, then act accordingly to effectively correct them.

Areas of concern include the following:

☑ Is your child being bullied?

☑ Is your child a bully?

☑ Is one child bullying another in your own home?

Pay attention to the warning signs to determine if your child is being bullied or happens to be the Bully.

▷ PARENTS OF THE BULLY

WHAT ARE THE WARNING SIGNS?

As a parent, there is nothing worse than getting a call from a teacher, principal or another parent about your child's misbehavior. No one wants to raise a "mean kid". However, if you do get that call, the most important thing that you can do is to acknowledge it and take responsibility, if it is true. The following are some of the warning signs to be aware of:

☑ *Is your child mean to neighbors, friends or siblings in your presence?*

If your child has the ability to say mean and hurtful things to people while you are around, there is a good chance it could be worse when you are not around. Be sure to listen and hear how your child treats others. Does he play fair with others? Does he speak to his peers with respect?

☑ *Has another parent or teacher ever called with a complaint about mean or disrespectful behavior?*

If so, please try not to get defensive and LISTEN. It is never easy to hear negative things about our children.

☑ *Does your child bring home belongings that are not his/hers?*

Your child may be taking things from other students or threatening weaker students into giving him their belongings.

☑ *Do you hear your child bragging to his friends about his mean behavior?*

In many cases, kids will talk about their bullying behavior to other children. Sometimes this is just bravado, but often times they want the attention that their bullying behavior is getting them. They want their friends to know who is in charge.

YOUR CHILD, THE BULLY

Many experts say that no other role is more important than the role of the parent of the bully. This parent holds the key to unlock the epidemic problem of bullying.

The problem is often complex: the parent of the bully is often a bully him/her self. The adage "the apple doesn't fall far from the tree" certainly applies here.

Many parents of bullies will handle the situation appropriately by getting help for their child. However, this doesn't happen often enough. Too often the parent of the bully is unapproachable and immediately gets defensive. The parent will blame the victim, the school, the teacher, or the other parent. Obviously, this doesn't solve the problem and empowers the bully to continue his behavior.

If your child has ever been accused of being mean or bullying other children, you, the parent must have an open mind. The only thing worse than a bully is a parent in denial that his child is a bully, particularly since this attitude perpetuates the problem. Not only does the victim suffer, the bully suffers as well.

The following research should concern you. A 2001 study from the Office of Juvenile Justice and Delinquency Prevention shows that those who bully appear to be at greatest risk of experiencing the following:

☑ Have trouble making friends

☑ Lack of success in school

☑ Involvement in problem behaviors such as smoking and drinking

☑ Loneliness

☑ Increase in criminal activity

IS YOUR CHILD PHYSICALLY VIOLENT?

Help your child figure out where he learned this behavior. It is not natural or healthy for children to behave this way. Ask yourself the following questions:

☑ Is there violence in your home?

☑ Is there a sibling that is physically aggressive towards this child?

☑ Does your child watch violent television or video games?

☑ Does your child listen to music that has violent messages and song lyrics?

ARE YOU THE PARENT OF A MEAN GIRL?

Some questions to ask yourself:

☑ Has your daughter ever been called a "mean girl"?

☑ Is your daughter constantly involved in "drama" with her friends?

☑ Is it difficult for your daughter to hold onto her friends for a long time?

☑ Do you hear your daughter talk badly behind other's backs?

☑ Have other parents or school officials called complaining about your daughter's behavior or involvement in trouble?

It is difficult to step back and evaluate our daughters separate from ourselves. However, it is imperative to objectively assess the situation. Sticking your head in the sand WILL NOT help your daughter and can damage her chances later for healthy adult relationships.

We must be able to accept our daughters' weaknesses if we are ever going to be able to help them grow into healthy young women. Otherwise, we are doing them a disservice by hindering their emotional development. Your daughter needs to acknowledge her own behavior, even if she doesn't want to hear the truth. She has plenty of friends (that are probably scared to death of her) and desperately needs someone to guide her and be her parent, not another friend.

▷ PARENTS OF THE BULLIED

Several studies have been conducted to determine if there is, in fact, a temperament that children are born with that makes them behave differently when it comes to socializing with their peers and/or behaving like a "victim".

Child psychologist David Schwartz conducted a study of children drawn from eleven different schools, none of whom knew each other at the beginning of the experiment. He sorted them into 30 play groups each including, one popular, one neglected, two average and two socially rejected boys. He then monitored them with hidden cameras over a five-day period and watched them interact.

Even in the first two sessions, before the bully/victim situations developed, the children who showed themselves to be "victim kids" behaved submissively. "They made no attempts to influence or persuade their peers – no demands, requests or even suggestions about how or what they should all play." Basically, they let their peers "walk all over them" (Schwartz, 1998).

Many questions are posed regarding, "is this nature or nurture"? Are children born a certain way which may lead them to become bullied or are we raising a nation of weak children? Are we teaching our children to be "too nice" and thus creating a "victim mentality"? Are we creating a nation of "victims" that must behave well at all times and never stand up for themselves or create conflict?

Dr. Paul Coughlin (2007) states the following:

"The problem of timid living is perpetuated with the creation of timid children. Ominous research tells us that today's kids are more timid, risk-averse and anxiety-ridden than past generations. Fear, my fellow parents, is our newest babysitter, our most prominent child-care consultant. The reasons are many but one of the most misunderstood and under-reported is our nation's most pervasive preoccupation: overprotective parenting".

The concept of overprotective parenting, can lead to the creation of victim mentality in our children. When discussing the victim, we as parents cannot ignore this concept and must be willing to check our individual parenting styles.

WHAT ARE THE WARNING SIGNS?

Being labeled a victim can follow a child from year to year and is a difficult cycle to break. If you are concerned that your child may be a victim of bullying, here are some warning signs:

☑ Acts moody, sullen or withdraws from family interaction

☑ Becomes depressed

☑ Loses interest in school work or grades drop

☑ Changes in sleeping or eating habits

☑ Won't use the bathroom at school and holds it until he returns home

☑ Arrives home with lost or torn clothing and won't explain why

☑ Asks for extra money for lunch or supplies

☑ Refuses to go to school or often acts sick

☑ Wants to carry a protection item, such as a knife

▷ DIVORCE AND BULLYING

It doesn't take much research to know that divorce is devastating for children. Their lives are torn apart and they often have to choose one parent over the other. Most parents won't admit it, but unless parents work very hard at having a "good" divorce, children are caught in the middle and can become casualties of this war.

With "high conflict" divorce, parents battle over custody and other issues. In these severe cases, one or both of the parents are bullying the other while struggling for control of the children.

What the parent doesn't understand is that this unacceptable behavior is a model for bullying for the children.

The behavior that is exhibited by children going through a divorce ranges from depression to rage and may manifest itself at school and on the playground. Sometimes, with overwhelming sadness and anger, the child doesn't know where to put these feelings so he takes them out on others weaker than himself.

The parents hold the key.

PART NINE: BYSTANDER

▷ INTRODUCTION

JOHN'S STORY

"Kids were talking all day about a fight that was going to happen after school between two boys that didn't like each other. One of them was a pretty good friend of mine and I was scared and worried. All the kids were talking about it and it was spread around that if anyone told the teachers, they would get beat up as well. I was sick to my stomach all day and didn't know what to do. After school a crowd formed and the two boys went at it. I felt sick to my stomach and ran away. The next day I heard that my friend got really hurt. I felt terrible that I didn't say something to someone. I could have prevented my friend from getting hurt. I feel really bad about it. What if that were me and no one helped?"

-John – 5th grade bystander

DEFINITION

The definition of "bystander" from Random House is:

"a person present but not involved; chance spectator; onlooker"

STAND BY, DO NOTHING

There are many players in the drama of bullying. The bully

and the victim are the obvious players but what about the person that stands around watching and chooses to do nothing? The bystander is the player that watches the drama unfold, either afraid to get involved for fear of becoming the next victim or just unsure of what to do about it. Either way, the bystander has a large role in why bullies get away with hurting other children.

Bystanders vastly outnumber bullies and victims yet research proves time and time again that most bystanders do not intervene. By standing around and being part of the audience that encourages the bully, the bystander is actually one good reason that the bully continues. Although the bystander is supposedly a passive role, his sheer existence encourages the perpetrator who is now driven by the attention he is receiving.

Everyone has been a bystander at some point in time. Culturally, we learn at a young age from society, as well as from our parents, to "stay out of it, it's none of your business." At what point does it become our business?

Author Paul Coughlin asks the question:

"What happened to courage and integrity?"

Many parents are raising children who are passive, pleasant and malleable rather than innovative, proactive and bold.

Coughlin goes on to say:

"How often do we diagnose a behavior as cowardice? For instance, what do you say after your son tells you about a bullying he witnessed and did not intervene, just stood there with the group? Have you helped him figure out that the sludge-like feeling gumming up his soul is a result of cowardice? Do you explain that cowardice is a normal but insufficient response to seeing someone unjustly treated or cruelly humiliated?"

Many parents never broach the subject of cowardice with their children. We usually don't think about teaching our children to be brave and stick up for the underdog, we usually are worried about our children protecting themselves from danger, at any cost. But what cost is it to our children's souls if they don't stand up for what is right and watch out for the people around them? Not only is it our responsibility to give our children the tools to protect themselves, but also the tools to care for others as well.

Bystanding is not a passive role. By doing nothing, the bystander is making a statement that bullying is OK. The audience that watches the bullying take place fuels the behavior of the Bully. If no one was watching, would the Bully care enough to do it?

▷ WHY DO STRA~
STAND BY, DO NO~.

SIMPLY, WHY DO OTHERS FAIL TO INTERVENE?

Think about it....when was the last time that you witnessed a situation and the thought went through your head, "I should probably help that person!"?

Most of us do not know what to do in a crisis situation. We have been taught, more than likely, to "stay out of it" or "don't get involved".

Craig and Peplar's research (1997) concluded that many bystanders do not intervene because:

☑ Children know that adults expect them to support each other but find it difficult to do so in the reality of playground life

☑ There is a 'diffusion of responsibility' among the crowd

☑ They are concerned for their own safety and self-preservation (afraid they will become the next victim)

☑ They don't fully understand the process of bullying and don't have the knowledge or skills to intervene effectively, worrying they may make matters worse for the victim

WHY DO PEERS STAND BY, DO NOTHING?

Canadian researchers conducted several studies regarding peer involvement in bullying (Craig and Pepler, 1997). These studies determined that peers were involved in some way in 85% of playground bullying occurrences.

☑ 54% of peers spent their time passively watching the event

☑ 21% of peers actively supported the bully

☑ 25% of peers intervened on behalf of the victims

☑ Both boys and girls participated equally in interventions

☑ 75% of interventions were successful in stopping the bullying

The studies concluded that *"the problem of bullying is systemic, extending beyond the bully and the victim"*.

Like other types of aggression, bullying occurs within a greater social setting. The dynamics of each school environment, each peer group, and each playground are varied. One factor is consistent: Aggressive behavior is driven by the need for attention and power within the social milieu of any given environment.

The bystander does influence the string of events in the act of bullying. No one is powerless and the bystander usually does not recognize the power he has to prevent and stop bullying from continuing. By saying and doing nothing, the bully continues with the silent approval of all of the people around him.

Other countries such as England, Canada and Finland have conducted studies specifically geared towards the bystander's role in bullying.

"Bullying is seen to be a group phenomenon in which a variety of players contribute a number of roles, pressures and influences, either intentionally or unintentionally, and are substantially involved in playground bullying, whether as active participants or as bystanders who are unable or unwilling to act pro-socially."

They conclude that *"peer group power could be utilized more positively in school classrooms to put an end to bullying."*

▷ HOW TO EDUCATE THE BYSTANDER

Discuss the concept of the bystander and what it means.

Years of studies and concluding evidence prove that the bystander plays a significant role in the drama of bullying. We must reach out and educate students to take control and intervene in bullying situations.

Give your child the tools to help intervene if he hears or sees bullying.

Proactive and preventative interventions implemented at the individual, class, school and community level are imperative if we are ever going to witness a dramatic decrease in bullying in our schools and neighborhoods.

Programs should be implemented in each school so that teachers and administrators are educated about the process. If a bystander does go to a teacher for help and nothing happens, he most likely will not go for help again. There has to be a system in place to protect the bystander once he has asked for help. At this point, we are putting the bystander in an unsafe position, set up for retaliation by the bully.

☑ Talk to your kids about standing up for what is right and taking action instead of silently approving of something they know is wrong. Develop a plan for every family member that instills empathy and compassion for others.

☑ Show respect for authorities such as Teachers and Law Enforcement.

☑ Encourage your children to volunteer in your community. By helping others, they will learn an important sense of obligation to other people and begin to take the focus off themselves.

☑ Help them understand that standing around and watching someone get bullied is essentially approving that behavior.

Summary for Kids: Don't just watch or walk away, take a stand. Intervene if you can by telling the Bully to stop or report the incident to your Parents or school officials. Give the Bullied your support!

SUMMARY (AND AUTHOR'S NOTE)

When my own young son came home one day clearly upset about a friend being bullied at school, I then realized how being a bystander can be devastating to a child. My son felt helpless, afraid and awful that he did nothing to help his friend. It was at that point I realized that the bully and victim were not the only casualties in the epidemic of childhood bullying. The bystander was one as well.

I soon began teaching my son how to take care of himself as well as stand up for others.

It is everyone's responsibility to try and do the same.

**PART TEN:
ALLIES**

Types of Allies

▷ TYPES OF ALLIES

DEFINITION

An Ally is a person or group of people that join in an association with someone for a common purpose. An Ally can be a positive person such as a friend, acquaintance or teammate. An Ally can also be an accomplice to a negative person or situation, thus siding with the Bullied or Bully, either actively or inactively (Bystander).

THE BULLY'S ALLIES

This Ally is often a weak person who usually watches the bullying from a distance. He supports the Bully by subtly or actively cheering on the torment of the Bullied. This "guilty by association" Ally is considered a bad guy by doing the wrong thing.

THE BULLIED'S ALLIES

The peer or friend of the kid who is bullied has a critical role as backup for the victim. In fact, there IS power in numbers. If enough kids get tired of their peers being harassed and realize the potential power they have to stop it, these Allies can be the heroes of the story. Otherwise, they often remain scared Bystanders.

It's time to stand up for what's right.

PART ELEVEN: EDUCATORS

Introduction

Teachers and Principal

Administration

School Watchers

▷ INTRODUCTION

WHY IS BULLYING ON SUCH A LARGE SCALE?

Why, because bullying is covert, under the radar and adults seldom see it. The bully is a master at the subtle comments and threatening actions that go unnoticed. Many adults see physical "play" between boys and misinterpret it as "horseplay" or come up with the age old adage, "boys will be boys". Those beliefs and comments have gotten us where we are today: the isolated, but still very troubling incidents of angry boys who come to school and shoot at peers and teachers who have not protected them from years of "horseplay".

Another issue concerns the victim. Often the victim will not tell on the bully, fearing he will anger the bully and escalate the bullying. Also, the victim and bully are often confronted together so once again, the fear stricken victim will deny any wrongdoing.

In severe cases, when the bullying has been going on for a long time, the victim actually believes that he "deserves" the bullying.

▷ TEACHERS AND PRINCIPAL

THEIR GRADES

People in general love to put blame on others instead of taking responsibility themselves. In much of the literature, authors blame the schools for their lack of programs and follow through and urge teachers and administrators to get more involved in the prevention and elimination of bullying. This of course is a wonderful idea, however, who is actually responsible for implementing these programs at the school level?

How much more can we ask of our principals and teachers without providing the needed education, funding and support that goes along with our demands?

In interviewing several teachers and principals, what seems to be a common thread in the hopes of eliminating bullying at schools is *visibility.*

"In terms of helping to control bullying, visibility is the key. The more I can be out on the playground and accessible to children, teachers and parents, the better. Paperwork is secondary to the safety of the children in our school. Ideally,

each school should have a protocol for working with bullying
on their campus. Administrators need to work closely
with teachers, parents and students as a team in order to
eradicate this problem."   -Scott Y., Principal

Teachers and administrators agree that when an adult is
present, children bully less. So, are principals and teachers
expected to be on the playground and at lunch every day to
monitor our children? This is an unrealistic expectation.
With continued funding cuts in the area of education, how
can we expect to hire more adults to monitor our children?

The solution must entail the entire school program, its
educators and administrators working with parents.

▷ ADMINISTRATION

THEIR ROLE

While the Teachers and Principal are on the frontline, Administration officials are like the Commanders.

They set and enforce policies as part of a district-wide plan that affect the region, state, and ultimately the country.

Many schools are empowered to implement their own anti-bullying programs. However, the only way this problem will truly be eradicated to the best of our ability is to get the complete backing and support of the School Administrators.

Success will come only when a solid program or programs are designed, implemented and consistently monitored.

School Administration, we need you on board.

▷ SCHOOL WATCHERS

THEIR ROLE

Secondary Players takes various forms and are thrust into importance by "simply being there".

They include the Parent Helpers (usually in the classrooms), Playground/Lunch Monitors (usually Teachers and Parents), Janitors and any other adult on campus.

These Players are on the frontline, but are usually not trained, rarely aware of the bullying dynamics on campus.

These players need to be trained and held accountable for the safety of our children. They need to be the "eyes and ears" for the Teachers and Principals who cannot always be there at the most crucial moments.

To fully succeed, School Watchers must have a role in a comprehensive solution.

**PART TWELVE:
AUTHORITIES**

Professional Counselors

Law Enforcement

▷ PROFESSIONAL COUNSELORS

It is important to follow a chain of command at your school. Teachers and administrators should be aware of any trouble your child is having. If in fact you have gone through the appropriate channels and have not received the help you need, it may be time to involve a Professional Counselor.

It will be important to make sure that this counselor is licensed and is experienced dealing with children, adolescents and families. This group includes Licensed Clinical Social Workers (LCSW), Marriage and Family Counselors (MFT) and Psychologists (PhD).

The role of the counselor may vary depending on the needs of your child. The counselor may need to provide individual therapy, mediate a situation with another family, or intervene at the school level. Depending on the situation, many of the players such as the Bully, Bullied, Ally or Bystander may benefit from talking to a professional.

A comprehensive list of resources in your area should be provided by your school.

▷ LAW ENFORCEMENT

Bullying can quickly unravel into a violent situation. That violence can result in serious injuries, ones that may prompt the Bullied family to contact law enforcement.

The goal is to keep your child safe and stop the bullying. The more extreme cases, including some Cyber Bullying, often need the law to intervene in order for the problem to get resolved.

However, this should be the last resort, usually after all other options have been exhausted.

Sometimes, there is no other choice.

EXTREME CASES: OUR GREATEST FEAR

Across the country, extreme cases of bullying that have turned violent have been showcased and discussed in the media. From the Columbine tragedy to the "bullying of Billy Wolfe" story, we continue to listen to the effects that long term bullying has on our children.

In Fayetteville, AR, Billy Wolfe was bullied mercilessly for such duration that after years of trying unsuccessfully to get the administration of his school district to help, his parents finally turned to litigation in order to be heard.

In March of 2008, the Wolfes sued one of the Bullies and subsequently considered another lawsuit against the Fayetteville School District. Although likely not receiving much financially, they felt a critical point needed to be made: schoolchildren deserve to feel safe. (*New York Times, 2008*).

While many people have felt that moving from hall monitors to lawyers is an overreaction, litigation may be the only method for school districts to take the issue of bullying more seriously. The first step, however, is to bring to light the seriousness of the problem and how the epidemic of bullying in our country is the exact opposite of what our educational system should be allowing.

Dan Olweus, a Norwegian psychologist makes the point that bullying cannot be prevented unless the school (and preferably the community, city and state) have a zero tolerance policy towards all acts of bullying and that punishments be dispensed immediately and equally upon all. Any failure to report an act of bullying, any delay in reporting it, any inequity in its punishment can be interpreted as compliance with the bullying. Unfortunately, the nature of bullying is such that even a wink, or a half smile, can give the okay (*Olweus, 1997*).

If we tolerate bullying in any way, at school, on the Internet or in our homes, we are demonstrating our approval of it.

It's time to take a stand.

**PART THIRTEEN:
COMMUNITY**

Influencers

Organizations and Corporate America

▷ INFLUENCERS

Kids in crisis, families in crisis, schools in crisis, all translate to a society in crisis.

As we agonize over the heartbreaking stories we hear on the news, most of us want to help but have no idea where to start.

There is a role for the rest of us; whether you have a child in the school system or not, you can make a difference. The most effective people in this group are the community leaders such as council representatives, religious leaders, coaches and other parents that interact with our children.

The community leaders must take the lead to promote child safety with a Bully-free environment in our schools. We can make changes and influence others to do the same.

We are all in this together.

▷ ORGANIZATIONS AND CORPORATE AMERICA

There are many organizations that can influence our society in a positive way, including the Boys and Girls Clubs of America, Boy and Girl Scouts, the Little League, etc.

Corporate America can offer monetary support for these programs, while helping to provide local and national exposure to promote safety in our schools.

Dignity and integrity must be restored in our homes, schools and playgrounds.

These Players ARE critical influencers.

PART FOURTEEN: BULLEAVE™

Introduction

10 Steps to Success

The BULLEAVE Mentor Program

The Big Dream

BULLEAVE WILL NOT ALLOW OTHERS TO DERAIL THE MAGIC OF CHILDHOOD

BULLEAVE™
WE CAN DO IT TOGETHER

▷ **10 STEPS TO SUCCESS**

STEP 1 **UNDERSTAND THE PROBLEM**
STEP 2 **KNOW BULLEAVE'S GOALS & OBJECTIVES**
STEP 3 **IDENTIFY SCHOOL PARTICIPANTS, DEFINE ROLES**
STEP 4 **DEFINE APPROACH & PLAN**
STEP 5 **EDUCATE PARTICIPANTS**
STEP 6 **EDUCATE PARENTS**
STEP 7 **IDENTIFY OUTSIDE RESOURCES**
STEP 8 **MONITOR & ADJUST**
STEP 9 **INVOLVE THE COMMUNITY**
STEP 10 **COMPONENTS FOR SUCCESS**

▷ BULLEAVE™ INTRODUCTION

BELIEVE THERE IS STILL A PROBLEM...AND MAKE THE BULLY LEAVE.

Numerous anti-bullying programs have consistently failed in their attempts to control or eliminate bullying. While no one expects bullying to completely disappear, most efforts attempt to lessen, not eliminate the problem.

BULLEAVE aims higher.

Some anti-bullying programs are complex while others are expensive and unwieldy. Most schools do not have the resources to make these programs work.

Meanwhile, society needs to find a comprehensive solution to bullying. Our children are victims of this *personal terrorism,* often finding themselves with little hope to make things right and regain their joyful childhood. The prevailing idea that "boys will be boys" must stop once and for all.

BULLEAVE has the answers.

BULLEAVE is a zero tolerance anti-bullying program that is ideally executed as team. However, it can be launched by a single concerned parent, teacher or administrator.

BULLEAVE educates and empowers.

BULLEAVE *educates* with a straightforward, comprehensive and inexpensive curriculum. It *empowers* those who lead the program with tools and a process that is easily implemented in schools. It is administered and monitored with intense scrutiny. It also successfully uncovers the truth, rewards the good and reforms the bad, with the hope and reconciliation needed to teach, heal and positively move forward to *eliminate* bullying.

BULLEAVE is different and powerful .

BULLEAVE addresses the root cause, confronts the reality, and provides a wide range of resources to help correct the problem. This program changes cultural environment and mindsets. It starts on a personal level and emerges on a national level.

What are you waiting for? Get started now.

▷ STEP 1 UNDERSTAND THE PROBLEM

The first step in BULLEAVE is becoming informed. Read the book GETTING BULLIED to truly appreciate and understand that a serious problem exists.

These facts are true.

☑ The problem of bullying is prevalent and undiminished

☑ There are children all around you who are suffering for no good reason

☑ There are other children who are acting out of control and cannot find the right help to stop

☑ Too little is done to fix the problem in our schools, to protect the innocent and to reform the bullies

▷ STEP 2 KNOW BULLEAVE'S GOALS & OBJECTIVES

☑ Stop, then reform the Bully

☑ Protect, then strengthen the Bullied

☑ Help the Bystander play an active role

☑ Educate all the players

☑ Empower the school for Zero Tolerance of Bullying

☑ Put a program in place that lasts

☑ Have a program that positively impacts society

▷ STEP 3 IDENTIFY SCHOOL PARTICIPANTS, DEFINE ROLES

Implementing a successful school program depends on solid involvement with key participants and leaders. The list potentially includes the following participants:

SCHOOL DISTRICT

SCHOOL ADMINISTRATION

PTA

TEACHERS, SCHOOL WATCHERS AND STUDENTS

School District

Ideally, the regional and/or local School District supports the program on all levels, eventually implementing it in all schools under its supervision.

PRESENTATION

BULLEAVE's program components and its benefits must be

presented to administrators, allowing them to suggest improvements that best fit the goals and objectives of the district. The district endorsement should open the doors to the schools themselves.

School Administration

The program succeeds with the full support of School Administrators. Set an appointment at the school (Principal/ Assistant Principal) to review the district meeting, layout the program's components and benefits, and suggest a plan to educate others at the school, including the Teachers, Students and School Watchers.

Discuss the hopes for soliciting help from the PTA once the Principal endorses the program.

PRESENTATION

BULLEAVE's components and its benefits must be presented, emphasizing the simplicity of the program and that minimal responsibilities will be asked of his staff.

DISTINGUISHED SCHOOL AWARD

Many schools apply for "Distinguished School" awards and will require this type of training and community involvement as part of the application process. Implementing BULLEAVE is an excellent way to meet this criteria. While the training can be considered staff development, the improved behavior and attitude of the students will benefit the entire school.

MONITORING

Progress will be monitored on an ongoing basis and results will be provided to School Administration, Teachers and Parents when appropriate.

WHAT IF THE PRINCIPAL DOES NOT PARTICIPATE?

If the Principal is hesitant or non-supportive, ask why. Are there components of the program that he does not agree with, etc? The beauty of the BULLEAVE Program is its ability to be customized to fit any situation or environment. Explain that you will work directly with him and his staff to meet his and his school's specific needs.

If the Principal is still unsure or non-supportive, ask for his permission to take it to the PTA or an outside community sponsor. At this point, if you still hit a roadblock, you may have to go to the district for support or even offer a variation of the program in the community (i.e. teacher, parent and student training).

Don't give up! The bullying of our children must be stopped. Roadblocks to a program's success will be overcome if you and your team are willing to persevere. Most Principals and Administrators will participate, understanding there is a real problem and a good plan to fix that problem.

PTA

Once the principal has approved the program, it is important to contact the PTA (Parent-Teacher Association) with your Plan. This group of concerned, active parents can be instrumental in ensuring the program's success.

The PTA may choose to appoint a position on the board for your anti-bullying program and even include it under their auspices. This will give the program additional credibility and support, as well as better access to Parents and Teachers.

PRESENTATION

Include in your presentation to the PTA that this program can be piloted at your school and receive recognition for community involvement and outreach.

PARTICIPATION

If the PTA supports the program but is not willing to participate or create a position on their board, that is not a roadblock. However, their awareness of this program soon to be implemented on your campus will still be valuable.

Teachers, School Watchers and Students

Teachers, School Watchers and Students will be introduced to the program in an assembly. There will be separate training for the Teachers and School Watchers, later classroom and assembly training for the Students.

The acceptance of these active participants will be monitored on an ongoing basis to ensure success.

Defining Roles

Once the participants have been identified, their roles will be defined. If the School District is on board, they may actively help define the district-wide program. If the School Administration supports the program, they should define their school's specific approach. If the PTA intends to get involved, their participation should make it easier to access the Parents.

The Teachers, School Watchers and Students will help ensure the Bully is exposed and reformed along with rewards and consequences to further help the Bullied.

▷ STEP 4 DEFINE APPROACH & PLAN

Once the participants have been identified and their roles have been defined, it is time to take the program and customize it to the specific needs of the school. It is important to encourage other parents alongside teachers to be a part of a *BULLEAVE Committee* and begin to operate as a "team" with the other participants.

If not actually blocked by school officials, the program can still be successfully developed and implemented by even one concerned parent or teacher

The author is available for consultation and guidance to help you get started.

The Plan

This roadmap to success must have certain components in order to succeed, including:

☑ Reasonable timeframes to implement

☑ Confirm responsibilities

☑ Solidify the education plan for participants

☑ Determine Rules, Rewards & Consequences

☑ Agree upon the regular monitoring timeframes

☑ All other Details

▷ STEP 5 EDUCATE PARTICIPANTS

Training the Teachers, School Watchers, Administration and Students is an essential element of the BULLEAVE program. Training should be complete, meaningful, yet concise.

While many programs overwhelm teachers with more tasks to complete, the primary goal of BULLEAVE is to integrate learning about bullying while promoting positive change in behavior both in the classroom and playground, making everyone's life easier with the least amount of effort.

TOPICS

The following will be covered in BULLEAVE training:

- ☑ Discussion of bullying types
- ☑ Long term effects of bullying
- ☑ How bullying affects education
- ☑ How bullying will be defined at your school
- ☑ Appropriate Rewards & Consequences
- ☑ Interventions with Principal and Parents as needed
- ☑ Distribution of questionnaire and follow up procedures

Teacher/School Watcher/ Administration Training (Outline)

1. Discuss the concerns and prevalence of bullying at their school as well as their own concepts of bullying.

2. Provide definitions of the Players:

> Types of Bullies (Typical, Sibling, Cyber, Girl)
> Victim/Target
> Bystander
> Parents (Bully and Bullied)

3. Brief discussion about the long term effects of bullying as stated throughout the book:

> Increased criminal-type behavior from the Bully
> Increased depression, anxiety and low self-esteem for the Bullied
> Issues of depression and guilt for the Bystander
> Other effects for friends, family and community

4. Empower these participants to take back control of their Students and their school by implementing BULLEAVE. Try to engage some Teachers to be on the BULLEAVE Team with the Parents.

5. Discuss the brief questionnaire and the protocol for distribution, Teacher meeting and interventions.

6. Review Rewards & Consequences that have been approved by the Principal and the BULLEAVE Team (see the list of options for schools to choose from as part of their own customized program that best fits their school's philosophy).

7. Discuss follow up questionnaire that will be distributed three months after BULLEAVE is implemented.

8. Thank the Teachers for their participation and support of the program. Make sure to discuss one of the main goals of this program, to restore safety and structure to their classrooms which will ultimately lead to a better learning environment for all students.

REWARDS & CONSEQUENCES*

The Rewards & Consequences component of BULLEAVE is open to new and different ideas from the teaching staff. The teachers are familiar with the students and may be able to define a more effective way to motivate the students at their school.

*Although the following is a basic escalation plan, if the first offense is severe, i.e. ANY physical contact, the plan must *implement an equally severe consequence such as immediate parent notification with suspension.*

Documentation of ALL offenses, no matter the severity, is mandatory.

CONSEQUENCES
First Offense

Verbal warning by Teacher or School Watcher and documentation of incident for future reference (unless the violation is severe enough to skip to more comprehensive action).

Second Offense

Receives lunch detention at a designated table and/or has to pick up trash at lunch instead of interacting with peers. Document incident.

Third Offense

Meeting with Principal and call home to Parents. Another lunch detention and final warning.

Fourth Offense

By now, the problem is severe enough to intensify the

consequences, including a Parent meeting that helps designate a behavior contract for the violator at home and at school.

Keep in mind that since BULLEAVE is in place, the Bully is now targeted and his bad behavior will be immediately challenged.

AGAIN, CONSEQUENCES ARE MOSTLY DETERMINED BY ACTION SEVERITY, NOT NECESSARILY QUANTITY OF OFFENSES.

REWARDS

It is important to reward good behavior. Below are a few ideas of what kinds of behavior merit rewarding:

- ☑ If a student reports a bullying incident, whether he was involved or simply a bystander
- ☑ If a student that once initiated a bullying incident changes his behavior
- ☑ If a peer or group of peers get actively involved in supporting BULLEAVE

Rewards can come in many forms such as:

- ☑ Homework pass
- ☑ Early out pass (5-10 minutes)

☑ Treat (donated by PTA or parent)

☑ Recognition at a student assembly

☑ Gift card (small amount) from a local store or community-based corporate sponsor

Student Training (Outline)

At a designated time, each teacher will hold a classroom discussion on bullying that has been provided by the BULLEAVE team. These are the pre-determined topics from the outline provided to each teacher.

The definition of bullying and different types of bullying will be discussed.

Teachers are expected to generate classroom discussion while setting up school-wide Rules for future appropriate behavior.

Students are informed that BULLEAVE is being implemented at their school, including explaining the Rewards & Consequences within the program.

Each teacher will be provided a simple Questionnaire to distribute to the students immediately following the discussion. This strategically-coordinated release will ensure students do not talk amongst themselves and potentially change their answers. The questionnaire will help to evaluate the extent of bullying at the school. The questionnaire is both uncomplicated and anonymous and includes the following questions:

☑ Have you ever been bullied at this school?

☑ Was the bullying physical, verbal or both?

☑ When and where did it occur?

☑ Have you ever been scared to come to school?

☑ Does the bully bother other children as well?

☑ Have you ever told a teacher or other adult about the bullying?

☑ Do you feel that you can talk to an adult at this school about the bullying?

☑ Can you share the name of the bully? (Remember, this information will be kept completely confidential, simply used by the school to help stop this unacceptable behavior).

Another component that can positively supplement BULLEAVE is Peer Training, helping train student leaders to positively influence other students. This can also extend to an even more "Powerful Allies" approach, building a wave of anti-bullying at the student level.

1. Begin discussion about bullying by asking Students about their impressions of the subject, types of Bullies, is there a problem at their school, where does it happen, and any ideas of how to stop it.

2. Discuss specifics on the types of Bullies, including Typical, Girl, Cyber and Sibling.

3. Discuss the different Players, including the Bully, Bullied, Bystander, Parents and all the school-related Players.

4. Discuss the importance of feeling safe at school and how BULLEAVE is going to be implemented. Let them know there is going to be ZERO tolerance of bullying behavior in the classroom and on the playground. This is for the safety and well-being of every student at school.

5. Discuss rewards and consequences that will be immediately implemented.

6. Distribute questionnaire and make it clear that it is anonymous. Make sure the students do not put their names on the paper.

7. Let the Students know that if there is anything they need to talk about regarding bullying, they can talk to you at any time.

▷ STEP 6 EDUCATE PARENTS

Parent Awareness is important to help start reforming the Bully or protecting the Bullied.

A comprehensive note will be provided to all parents by the BULLEAVE Team to help educate them about the Program.

There is also a Parent Education Night organized by the BULLEAVE team or a consultant/therapist.

Parents will also be able to work with the Teachers and Administration to complete the circle.

After an incident, the school may initiate communication with the parents, ensuring the parents are well-aware of the problem and solutions.

▷ STEP 7 IDENTIFY OUTSIDE RESOURCES

Sometimes, solutions to the problems require additional expertise and other resources outside of the school and home. It usually depends on the type and severity of the problem.

These resources can include therapists and licensed clinical social workers to assist individuals and families in coping with the effects of bullying as well as helping with finding answers for the future.

There are support groups who are either available today or can be organized as a discussion and solution resource.

When the problem gets out of control, possibly with criminal aspects, law enforcement can be invaluable.

The role of the BULLEAVE Coordinator is to identify, compile and distribute a list of these local resources to the school and homes. The primary objective is to plug any holes that might exist, ensuring that there is help at any level to eradicate the problem once and for all.

▷ STEP 8 MONITOR AND ADJUST

IN MOTION

The program has been put into motion. Now is the time to get more specifics about the school environment to determine if BULLEAVE is succeeding in making a difference.

After collecting the questionnaires, each grade level will conduct a team meeting and the "at risk" children will be identified. This confidential information will only be discussed between Teachers and Administration, excluding the parent volunteers for critical privacy reasons.

Questionnaire results will also identify problem areas on the school ground, such as bleachers and bathrooms. Students who need intervention will also be identified and helped.

Confirm that everything is in process, that all participants are in place, and that results will be forthcoming.

RESULTS

At this time, the program follows through with Rewards & Consequences. All BULLEAVE team members have the same protocol to follow for dealing with bullying and the aftermath. Volunteer supervision may be needed to oversee areas that have been targeted as "unsafe" in the questionnaire.

There will be Post-Incident tracking, including the mandatory Incident Report documented with the school. This report can be initiated by any player, detailing names, proof, and eyewitness accounts that will be compiled in the school database of those involved to better determine patterns.

There will also be an effort to "repair the damage", helping the Bullied and the Bully. This is an important step in the healing process for both parties.

Follow-up Program Reviews will also take place quarterly with all the key participants on the team. The Program will be amended as necessary.

Follow-up questionnaires will be distributed quarterly to each student in order to assess BULLEAVE's effectiveness.

MAKE CHANGES

By now, BULLEAVE has had time to match schoolyard reality with a full process in motion. There is an opportunity to apply measurements to specifics, determining if the results

146

thus far suggest a successful implementation of the program.

Even with success, there is always room to tweak and improve. The Committee should meet and find ways to make BULLEAVE better. The goal is an airtight program that does not allow failure. Zero tolerance.

▷ STEP 9 INVOLVE THE COMMUNITY

The community at large must be made aware of the pervasive problem of childhood bullying.

Setting up a meaningful partnership at the Community level for anti-bullying can be powerful and society-changing. This may include sports clubs, religious organizations and our neighborhoods.

There is also great hope that the corporate world will work in conjunction with the schools and families to ensure total success.

▷ STEP 10 COMPONENTS FOR SUCCESS

Powerful results will be more attainable if you take inventory of the true components for success:

TEAMWORK

CORRECTLY GAUGING SEVERITY AND ACTING ACCORDINGLY

COMPLETENESS

CHANGE BEHAVIORS, CREATE A NEW CULTURE

FOCUS ON A LASTING SOLUTION

IMPLEMENT WITH SPEED AND PRECISION

OFFER TRUST, HOPE AND COMFORT

A MAJOR SHIFT OF POWER TOWARDS GOOD

IT'S ALL ABOUT ZERO TOLERANCE

BULLEAVE WILL NOT ALLOW OTHERS TO DERAIL THE MAGIC OF CHILDHOOD

▷ THE BULLEAVE MENTOR PROGRAM

Who better to turn to than our own children?

Children and teenagers that are bullied often have nowhere to go and no one to turn to. While they need to feel loved and supported by the adults in their lives, healthy peer relationships are equally as important. The BULLEAVE Mentor Program focuses on helping a younger child who may be struggling socially or being bullied by connecting him with an older, more confident child. The peer leaders should be trained to resolve conflict, help prevent young people from being bullied, while providing support and advice in order to help these other students Students may have peer mentors who have a history of bullying themselves.

Overall, the BULLEAVE Mentor Program promotes positive interaction between peers and younger students, ultimately helping build a safer campus.

THE BIG DREAM

We can all dream big about eradicating bullying for our children throughout the country, but we must also be willing to do it one school at time, one child at a time. If each administrator supports each teacher, and each teacher supports each family and each family supports their kids and other kids support their peers...we can all make a difference in the lives of our most precious treasures, our children.

Aren't our children worth it?

**PART FIFTEEN:
ENFORCE
CHILDHOOD
JUSTICE**

Going Nationwide

▷ ENFORCE CHILDHOOD JUSTICE

THE LACK OF PRINCIPLE BY A PRINCIPAL

GETTING BULLIED deals with bullying on a personal level, and then asks the schools, parents and community to take charge and fix this serious problem. One option is to implement an anti-bullying program like BULLEAVE. If for some reason that is not possible, then those in charge are expected to effectively take care of problems one incident at a time.

What happens when an anti-bullying program is not in force and a school and its entire school district badly mishandles a serious bully situation by brushing the facts under a table stacked with denials? Even worse, what if that school and school district follow those denials with blackmail? It happens more than you know.

In 2008, a middle school in Southern California allowed the unthinkable to happen. A young boy became a constant victim of bullying until he was eventually hit over the head, losing consciousness and breaking both arms upon falling to the ground.

The school had an ideal opportunity to fix one obvious and serious bullying situation, but instead chose to operate on a low integrity plane and ignore it, deny it, and then attempt to blackmail the mother with a small amount of money in order to release the school of any responsibility.

This single, financially strapped mother was forced to pay all the medical bills herself. She then hired an attorney in order to obtain justice. However, this is NOT justice.

Justice expects all parties to operate with decency, integrity and fairness from the beginning, period. If a school administrator or even worse, an entire school district cannot operate within that clearly defined realm of honesty and decency, they join the bully in becoming perpetrators of injustice. Actually, they are much worse.

People in power must be held accountable by its citizens. Most importantly, suffering families who agonize over abuse of their children at the hands of a bully must never be further victimized by the lack of principles of a school system.

The consequence must be even harsher on school authorities who appear to be aligning with the bully. Not only does this horrendous injustice warrant job termination, legal, and even criminal charges must be filed against those who let down our children.

BULLEAVE stands for eliminating childhood injustices at the hands of bullies, and eliminating poor actions or inaction of those in power. If our laws are not strong enough to prosecute the guilty and protect the innocent, then the laws must be changed.

BULLEAVE is also prepared to extend its own responsibilities beyond implementing its simple, yet comprehensive zero tolerance anti-bullying school effort.

The only way to enforce zero tolerance is to believe in zero tolerance and BULLEAVE is going to take action to ensure these goals are met and get involved with any and all bullying situations presented to the program. Each situation will be presented to the right authorities with the expectation that the good guys will be protected and the bad guys will be exposed and reformed, all part of a total resolution of the problem.

The author and the BULLEAVE team can be reached at shininglion@cox.net or through the website www.GettingBullied.com.

APPENDIX + INDEX

✓ BIBLIOGRAPHY

Ball, Sue (2007) *Bystanders and Bullying.* Retrieved March 16, 2008, from http://www.anti-bullyingalliance.org.uk

Barry, D.(2008, March 24) The boy the bullies love to beat up, repeatedly. *The New York Times,* pp. A1-A4.

Bullying Facts and Statistics. Retrieved December 27, 2007 from http://www.safeyouth.org

Coloroso, Barbara. (2003) *The Bully, the Bullied and the Bystander.* New York, NY: Harper Collins.

Coughlin,Paul. (2007) *No More Jellyfish, Chickens or Wimps.* Minnesota: Bethany House Publishers.

Craig,W. and Peplar, D. (1997) *Observations of bullying and victimization in the school years.* Canadian Journal of Psychology,2, 41-60.

Fox, M. (2007). *Teens take bullying to the Internet, study show.* Retrieved November 23, 2008 from http://www.reuters.com.

Harding,A. (2007). *Most primary school children report being bullied.* Journal of Developmental and Behavioral Pediatrics,3, 22-24.

Kelly, M. (2005) *What if your child IS the bully?* Retrieved February 12, 2008 from http://www.pacer.org.

Knoll, K. (2001) *Bullying statistics.* Retrieved December 30, 2007 from http://www.endthehate.org.

Merriam-Webster's collegiate dictionary (10th edition).(1993). Springfield, MA: Merriam Webster

Olweus, Dan. (1993) *Bullying at school: What we know and what we can do.* Oxford: Blackwell.

Patchin, J.W. and Hinduja, S. (2006) *Bullies move beyond the schoolyard: A preliminary look at cyberbullying.* Youth Violence and Juvenile Justice, 4(2), 148-169.

Schifferdecker, S. *Sibling Rivalry.* Retrieved January 23, 2007 from http://www.More4Kids.com. More4Kids

Schwartz,D. (2000). *Subtypes of Vicims and Aggressors in Children's Peer Groups.* Journal of Abnormal Child Psychology, 28, 181-192.

Simmons, Rachel. (2001). *Odd Girl Out: The hidden culture of girls' aggression.* San Diego, Ca.: Harcourt Brace.

Stopcyberbullying, Retrieved March 3, 2008 from http://www. stopcyberbullying.org.

Tarshis, T (2007). *Psychometric Properties of the Peer Interactions in Primary School Questionnaire,* Journal of Developmental and Behavioral Pediatrics.

Turley, J. (2008, July 15). *Bullying's Day in Court.* USA Toda, 135, 28-31.

Wiseman, Rosalind. (2002). *Queen Bees and WannaBees.* New York: Random House.

✓ RESOURCES

WEBSITES

http://stopbullyingnow.hrsa.gov/index.asp?area=main

http://kidshealth.org/teen/your_mind/problems/bullies.html

http://www.safeyouth.org/scripts/topics/bullying.asp

http://www.stopcyberbullying.org/index2.html

http://www.bullying.org

http://www.bullyingcourse.com

http://www.kidshelp.com

http://www.anti-bullyingalliance.org.uk

http://www.ncab.org.au (National Centre Against Bullying, NCAB)

http://www.nea.org/schoolsafety/bullying.html?mode=print

BOOKS

Coughlin, Paul (2007) No More Jellyfish, Chicken or Wimps

Wiseman, Rosalind (2002) Queen Bees and Wannabees

Simmons, Rachel (2002) Odd Girl Out

Coloroso, Barbara (2003) The Bully, the Bullied and the Bystander

✓ INDEX

✓ ABOUT THE AUTHOR

Katie Mann, LCSW, author of GETTING BULLIED, received her undergraduate degree in Psychology from University of California, Los Angeles. She then completed her graduate studies in Social Work at California State University, Long Beach with an emphasis in Children, Youth and Families. Currently in private practice in San Clemente, California, Katie has been a keynote speaker at many schools and organizations on the topics of Bullies, Cliques and Myspace. She resides in San Clemente with her husband and two children. For more information on her work, visit www. GettingBullied.com.

Author's Acknowledgements

Finally, my passion put into words. This book has been a long time coming and I would like to thank all of my family, friends and colleagues who encouraged me to persevere. Your support and love mean everything.

I would most importantly like to thank my sweet husband Tim and wonderful kids, Molly and Joe. Throughout this journey, they never wavered in their love and support of this project. I truly could not have done it without them.

In conclusion, I hope this book matters. I hope it will help make the changes desperately needed to protect our precious children from these childhood injustices.